C

D0643933

WITHDRAWN

SPEEDBOAT RACERS

Michael Hauenstein

Enslow Publishers, Inc.
40 Industrial Road
Box 398
Berkeley Heights, NJ 07922
USA

http://www.enslow.com

Library of Congress Cataloging-in-Publication Data
Hauenstein, Michael.
  Speedboat racers / Michael Hauenstein.
    p. cm. — (Kid racers)
  Includes bibliographical references and index.
  Summary: "High interest book for reluctant readers containing action packed photos and stories of the hottest speedboats and races for kids, discussing which boats qualify, how they are built and raced, who the best drivers are, what to look for in a powerboat, safety, good sportsmanship, and how racing activities can be a good part of family life"—Provided by publisher.
  ISBN 978-0-7660-3485-3
  1. Motorboat racing—Juvenile literature. I. Title.
  GV835.9.H38 2010
  797.1'4—dc22
                          2009020787

ISBN 978-0-7660-3755-7 (paperback)

Printed in the United States of America

102009 Lake Book Manufacturing, Inc., Melrose Park, IL

10 9 8 7 6 5 4 3 2 1

To Our Readers:
We have done our best to make sure all Internet addresses in this book were active and appropriate when we went to press. However, the author and the publisher have no control over and assume no liability for the material available on those Internet sites or on other Web sites they may link to. Any comments or suggestions can be sent by e-mail to comments@enslow.com or to the address on the back cover.

Any stunts shown in this book have been performed by experienced drivers and should not be attempted by beginners. Proper training is needed before attempting to drive a race boat.

♻ Enslow Publishers, Inc., is committed to printing our books on recycled paper. The paper in every book contains 10% to 30% post-consumer waste (PCW). The cover board on the outside of each book contains 100% PCW. Our goal is to do our part to help young people and the environment too!

Adviser: *Mark Wheeler, vice president, American Power Boat Association*

Cover Photo Credit: APBA/Roland Dechert
Interior Photo Credits: APBA/Bill Taylor, p. 5; APBA/Teri Ziemer, p. 7; APBA/Jean Tennell, pp. 11 (bottom), 24, 33, 38, 40; APBA/Leo Schlotter, p. 19; APBA/Mike Johnson, p. 28; APBA/Roland Dechert, p. 32; APBA/D'Agostino family photo, p. 37; AP Photo, p. 8; Fotolia/Kushnirov Avraham, pp. 42–43 (background); Getty Images, pp. 30, 31; Getty Images/AFP/Jeff Kowalsky, p 36; Patrick Gleason, pp. 11 (top), 18, 19, 22, 35, 42, 43; Mary and Andy McGavic, pp. 13, 20, 21 (bottom), 27, 39; The Norwegian Emigrant Museum, negative # U01191, p. 9; Michael Price, pp. 4, 6, 12, 15, 16, 17, 21 (top), 23, 25, 26, 29; Racine Extreme/T. Oleson, p. 41; Kevin Tombs, p. 14.

Contents

SPEED AND SPRAY

You've probably traveled at 40 miles per hour before. In the comfort of a car or a train, you may *think* you know what that speed feels like. But to a speedboat racer, kneeling in a small cockpit just inches above the surface of the water, 40 mph feels very different.

In the Cockpit

Imagine skimming across the water, heading for the starting line, with eleven other speedboats beside you. Your engine revs behind you. The race has begun.

The crowd on the shoreline cheers as you speed toward the first turn. Suddenly, a wall of white water blurs your vision—the water is spraying off the other boats as they turn, too. You quickly find the bright orange buoys that mark the turn. You squeeze the throttle, and your engine revs again as you plan your course for the next straightaway.

You are a speedboat racer.

The Main Event

Junior class racers run as many laps and as many races as adult boat racers. The junior races are just as popular with fans, too!

Teen racer Tyler Welch worked his way up through the junior classes. Here, he takes a quick break at an event in Champlin, Minnesota. Welch wears a life jacket that keeps him afloat and protects his body and neck.

WHO CAN RACE?

You can start racing powerboats at the age of nine.
It doesn't matter if you're a boy or a girl, tall or short, big or small. Successful boat racers come in all shapes and sizes.

Rookie Rules

You must take a written test before you can race in the junior classes of the American Power Boat Association (APBA). Rookie drivers wear white crosses on their helmets. This shows they are beginners.

A junior-class racer keeps his focus during an event in Poplar Grove, Illinois.

Left to right: Lauren Johnson, Ashley Rucker, Wendy Eldredge, and Amy Nydahl pose at the 2008 APBA Professional Racing Outboard Nationals. Nydahl was inducted into the APBA Hall of Champions at the age of eleven.

Racing Up the Ranks

The maximum age for the junior classes is fifteen. Many kids start racing in the faster adult classes when they reach high school. For example, you can race a 65-mph boat by the time you turn sixteen. By your eighteenth birthday, you could be piloting an 80-mph hydroplane.

No Copilot Needed

Even the youngest boat racers pilot the boats by themselves. Drivers learn to make split-second decisions on their own during a race.

SPEEDBOAT RACING HISTORY

Motorboats first took to American waters in the late 1800s. Yacht clubs started to hold races on rivers and lakes. By the early 1900s, motorboat racing had official rules. It became a national sport.

A few years later, the outboard motor was invented. Outboards are lighter than the big car engines used in other race boats. Racers created different classes—groups of racers—for boats with different designs and engine sizes.

Motors in Stock

In the mid-1940s, the racing community added some new classes of outboard racing. They were called stock outboard classes because the motors came right from the factory, with no changes.

Gar Wood (left) was one of the first great boat racers. He also designed and built thousands of boats from the 1920s to the 1940s.

All Kinds of Boats

Today there are many types of race boats. Unlimited hydroplanes are boats powered by jet engines. Inboard hydroplanes are powered by car engines. Formula One tunnel boats use outboard engines to reach speeds of 140 mph. Huge offshore speedboats compete on the open ocean.

Racing with small outboards is still the most popular form of powerboat competition in the United States.

The First Outboard Motor

Ole Evinrude (right) invented the first widely sold outboard motor in 1909. He wanted something better than a rowboat. Once he rowed across a lake on a hot day to get ice cream for his girlfriend. He ended up with a soggy mess instead.

Organized Racing Begins

The American Power Boat Association was formed in 1903. Representatives of twenty yacht clubs held a meeting. They created a set of rules for racing.

HISTORY OF JUNIOR RACING

Junior boat racing began when stock outboard racing became popular in the late 1940s. This type of racing is done on a local level by amateurs who compete on a family budget.

Junior Speed

Engine and boat technology have changed over the years. The boats have become much faster. For example, in 1967, the top racing speed for juniors was 32 mph. In 1987, the fastest junior racer went 38 mph. Today's top speed record is 43 mph.

Racing Against Mom?

In the early days of junior hydroplane racing, it was sometimes hard to find enough kid racers. Mothers raced against the kids to give them more competition.

The competition in speedboat racing isn't just fast—it's *close*.
It's hard to believe that there are two boats in this picture!

Racers of Tomorrow

Today, there are junior classes in every racing
category. The leaders of the sport realize it is
important to teach kids how to race. After all,
kid racers will drive the next generation of high-
tech race boats in the future.

Top Kid Racer: Dylan Runne

There are two junior classes in boat racing. Dylan
Runne, a teenager from New Jersey, was a double
champion in 2008. Runne won the national
championship races and the end-of-season high
point standings in both junior classes.

**Boat racer Dylan Runne makes a speech
after entering the APBA Hall of Champions
in January 2009.**

5

Racers keep their eyes on a buoy (right) so they know where to turn.

GOING TO A RACE

Going to a boat race is a great way to learn about the sport. Boating Web sites, local racing clubs, and national racing organizations can help you find a race in your area.

At the Race

The racing community is friendly and close-knit. Talk to the drivers at the event. Ask them about their equipment, how they got into racing, and what it takes to get started.

A typical racecourse is shaped like an oval. The turn at each end is marked by a buoy.

You'll see a large clock on the judges' stand. The clock is used to start a kneel-down race.

The Action Begins

When the green flag flies from the judges' stand, it means the heat (racing round) starts in three minutes. The excitement builds as boats make their way onto the course. One minute before the start, the white flag flies. The clock starts to count down. The drivers jockey for starting positions. They want to cross the start/finish line at the moment the clock hits zero.

Each heat usually lasts three laps. The winner is the driver with the highest combined score from two heats of racing.

A white flag flies on the judges' stand at a race in Whitney Point, New York.

Don't Be a Gun Jumper

Sometimes drivers cross the starting line before the clock hits zero. These drivers are called gun jumpers, and they get no points for the heat. Race officials use a video camera to find gun jumpers.

GETTING STARTED

Most racing teams are made up of families. Parents and kids can race at the same events. Once you have your team together, the next step is to find the right equipment.

Watch the Pros

It's a good idea for beginners to get used to driving a boat in competition before spending money on brand-new equipment. You might find

At the 2008 Stock Outboard Junior Championships, a man helps his son prepare for a big race.

If you go to a boat race, ask drivers about the different types of boats. This will help you decide on what you want.

that your personal driving style matches up to a different boat than the first one you tried.

Buying a Boat

Most local racing clubs will let you borrow a boat to give racing a try. If you're ready to buy one, many good used boats are available. You can find them at a race, in magazines, or on the Internet. Experienced racers can tell you if you're getting a good deal. Don't be afraid to ask.

Newer Isn't Always Better

Many boat racers win with used equipment. Danielle Kobren of Pennsylvania won the 2003 junior hydroplane nationals in a boat that her uncle gave her. Kobren's uncle got the boat used, too!

This kid racer's boat has a big engine that provides plenty of power.

RACING EQUIPMENT

You only need four things to race a powerboat: a driver, a boat, safety gear, and an engine. The outboard engine mounts on the transom of the boat, at the back of the cockpit. The driver kneels in the cockpit. You can choose a padded cockpit floor or simply wear kneepads.

Ready, Set, Race!

Now, what do you do with your equipment? While kneeling, you work the throttle with your left hand to control the engine speed. The throttle is like a gas pedal for your hands. You grip the steering wheel with your right hand and lean out of the cockpit to make left-hand turns. On the left side of the boat is a turn fin that helps guide it through the turns.

How do you get your boat up to speed? Squeeze the throttle!

Weight Rules

Boat racing rules require drivers and their equipment to meet a minimum weight, but there is no maximum weight. Lightweight drivers add lead weights to their boats to meet the weight requirement.

17

HYDROPLANES AND RUNABOUTS

Hydroplanes and runabouts are the two types of boats used in junior racing. These two boats have different hull designs, so they feel completely different when you drive them.

Hydro-Power

A hydroplane has two sponsons on the front end. The sponsons look like small pontoons.

It takes skill to drive an outboard hydroplane at race speeds. Driver Ashley Rucker has to watch closely for other boats and changing conditions on the racecourse.

They help keep the boat on top of the water. A long fin called an air trap runs from each sponson to the tail end of the boat. Together the sponsons, the air traps, and the sleek shape of the boat allow hydroplanes to rise off the water and run on top of a pocket of air. This pocket of air keeps the boat free of the water, reduces drag, and allows the boat to reach top speeds.

Rough Riding

A runabout is a flat-bottom boat with a simple hull design. These wedge-shaped boats do not have sponsons or air traps. Instead, they have pointed bows. Runabouts are generally slower than hydroplanes, but they can move through rougher water. Many people think it takes more skill to drive a runabout.

Junior racer Braxton Miller drives a runabout in 2009.

A Boating Marathon

Marathon racing is a special type of boat racing for runabouts only. Runabout drivers race on narrow, winding rivers in rough water.

OUTBOARD ENGINES

A junior class race boat is powered by an outboard motor. That means the engine is clamped onto the transom—the back of the boat. The engine is light enough that you can remove it from the boat and work on it in your house or garage (with an adult's approval, of course).

Shown here is a stock Evinrude engine.

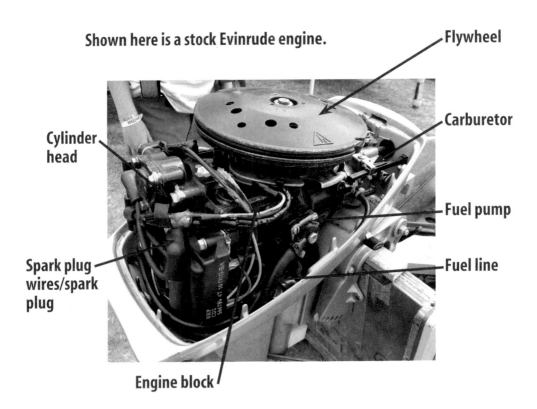

Flywheel

Carburetor

Cylinder head

Fuel pump

Fuel line

Spark plug wires/spark plug

Engine block

Firepower

An outboard motor is called an internal combustion engine because it burns gasoline to create power—just like most car engines. The engine takes in a mixture of gas and air. The spark plugs set the mixture on fire. This combustion moves the pistons, which turn the gears and shafts that spin the boat's propeller.

A race team member gases up his driver's hydroplane.

Engines of the Future

Soon, new technology will replace today's engines. Engines will continue to become better for the environment. In the future, junior racers might drive boats with electric engines. Anything is possible.

Fuel for Juniors

The gas tank on a junior race boat holds about 0.5 gallon of gas (right).

PROPELLERS

A powerboat needs a well-designed hull and a strong engine. But what actually makes the boat move through the water? The propeller, also called the prop.

Running on Blades

Propellers used in junior racing are made of stainless steel. Stainless steel is a type of metal that is strong and resists rusting. A typical junior racing propeller has three blades.

The prop is located at the back of the boat. It is attached to the lower portion of the outboard motor. The engine turns gears and shafts that make the propeller rotate. The shape of the prop's blades turns this rotation into forward propulsion. Just as a fan's blades pull air through the back and blow it out the front, a prop's blades pull water from the front and push it out the back. The action of the water moves a boat forward.

Most propellers are made of stainless steel, aluminum, or a composite (mixture of metals).

For Kids Only: Special Propellers

All the propellers used in junior boat racing are exactly the same. This keeps costs down and encourages fair competition. It's all about the skill of the driver.

SAFETY GEAR

When race boats are deck-to-deck at speeds close to 40 mph, there's always a chance that something could go wrong. A boat in front of you could stall or break down. A driver could lose control of his boat and hit yours. Someone could cut you off around a turn. To make sure nobody gets hurt, racers are required to wear safety equipment. This includes helmets, life jackets, and cut-resistant suits.

Dylan Runne (left) gets too much air under his boat. This is an accident waiting to happen.

In this high-speed sport, racers wear high-tech gear to stay safe.

Boat racing helmets are bright orange or yellow. This makes drivers easy to see both in and out of the water.

Life jackets protect drivers from impact and keep them afloat if they go overboard. Like helmets, life jackets are brightly colored.

A cut-resistant suit protects the driver's arms and legs from injury. It is made out of a material such as Kevlar or Spectra, just like a police officer's bulletproof vest. Your suit shields you from a collision with a propeller blade, turning fin, or other sharp object.

Protect Your Hands and Feet, Too

For added protection, boat racers wear gloves and socks made of cut-resistant material.

A rescue boat patrols the racecourse on Lake Sule in Illinois.

THE RESCUE CREW

At every race you'll see a large boat slowly patrolling the middle of the course. The people on this boat wear scuba diving gear, talk into handheld radios, and keep an eye on every boat on the water. This is the safety boat. It's not part of the race, but it's probably the most important boat at the event.

In an Instant

The safety boat stays in constant contact with the judges' stand and an ambulance on the shore. If anything goes wrong during a race, the rescue crew responds in an instant. If a junior racer enters the water for any reason, the race is stopped and the rescue crew springs into action.

On the Scene

First, the crew makes sure the driver is out of danger from other boats. Then they check to see if the driver is hurt. Sometimes they take the driver to the ambulance or medical station to get checked out. But most of the time the driver is okay—just soaking wet.

What Are Those Other Boats?

The race boats and the rescue boat aren't the only boats on the water during a race. Officials in patrol boats (below, foreground) watch for drivers who are breaking rules. They also tow stalled boats off the course.

SAFE DRIVING

The best way to stay out of accidents is to be aware of your surroundings at all times. It's not enough to pay attention to where you're going. You also have to keep an eye out for what other racers are doing.

Before the Flag

Most accidents happen before the race even starts! Just before the start of the race, drivers enter the course and make sure their equipment is working properly. They check out the course, take practice starts, and get in position.

Junior hydroplane drivers keep a safe distance between boats at the start of a race in Moses Lake, Washington.

Racers plan their strategies on Candlewick Lake in Illinois.

Some drivers forget to notice the other boats around them. If you don't pay attention, you could get in a crash.

During the Race

Once the race starts, there are two key ways to avoid accidents. First, hold your lane through the turns. Second, watch the flag signals. There are flags on the judges' stand and in patrol boats on the racecourse. They'll let you know if the race needs to be stopped. (Turn to page 44 to learn about all the flags and what they mean.)

Look Before You Turn!

Look over your shoulder before making a turn. This keeps you from cutting in front of another boat. Cutting someone off is dangerous—and it's against the rules.

ON COURSE

In boat racing, you never race on the same course twice. That doesn't mean you don't go to the same location more than once. You don't race on the same course twice because water conditions are always changing. Wind speed, wind direction, currents, tides, and the number of boats make the course different every time.

Bodies of Water

Races are held on different bodies of water throughout the world. The most common locations are freshwater lakes and rivers. The size and shape of the lake or river helps determine the size and shape of the course.

Offshore race boats take a turn in the harbor at the Key West Offshore World Championship in Florida.

Anything Is Possible

Can you imagine racing around an island? Or how about speeding under a bridge side by side with other racers? You have to be ready for anything when you race a boat.

A speedboat whizzes under two bridges during the Marathon Super Boat Grand Prix.

Working with Currents

A river with a strong current can make a boat run differently upstream than it runs downstream.

CHAMPIONSHIP RACES

Most junior racing happens in local towns. But during each racing season, there are a few national championship events. The biggest race of the season is the APBA Stock Outboard National Championships.

Racers from All Over
The national championships are held in a different place every year. They could be in California or Michigan, New York or Washington. Hundreds of racers enter for a chance to be the national champion.

The event is more than a race—it's a festival. Teams from around the country spend a full week at the race site. Television crews capture live broadcasts. The races are more intense than ever, and the trophies are bigger. It's a giant rush of energy.

Junior Champs

At the end of the year, racing officials declare champions for two junior classes: J Hydro and J Runabout. Bonus points are awarded for championship wins, but the local races still count for most of the points.

Winning racers pose at the Professional Racing Outboard World Championships in Lake Alfred, Florida, in October 2008. In the front row (left to right) are North American champion Andrew Thirlby, third-place driver Amy Nydahl, and second-place racer Becky Nichols.

Big Prizes for Juniors

Some really cool prizes are given out at the APBA National Championships. For example, junior racers might win a new boat or a new motor.

WHAT IT TAKES TO WIN

There's a saying in kneel-down boat racing: the race is won or lost on the start. It takes skill to time the clock start perfectly, and each heat lasts only a few laps. This is very different from car racing, where the race starts cleanly and lasts many laps.

Land Versus Water

Racing on water is different from racing on land. For example, in boat racing you need to find the shortest route around the course. Cars and other road racers use the whole track to keep their speeds up.

What's the Force?

Race boats have sleek designs that lift the boat off the water. Race cars, on the other hand, need a downward force to keep the car on the track

At top speeds, a driver crouches as low as he can to create less drag. This helps the boat fly even faster.

and in control. A boat driver can move forward or backward in the cockpit to make the boat lift off the water more or less. This skill takes practice but can make a big difference.

The Quickest Way Around the Course

In boat racing, acceleration—how quickly your boat speeds up—is more important than top speed.

WINNERS

Junior boat racers have gone on to race everything from huge, ocean-going offshore powerboats to Unlimited hydroplanes powered by jet engines.

Chip Hanauer (below) has won the most APBA Gold Cups in Unlimited hydroplane racing history. He is a member of the International

Motorsports Hall of Fame. Hanauer started his racing career in the junior hydroplane class in the Seattle area.

Mixing Sports

Kids who start out in boat racing succeed in other sports, too. Dallas Stars hockey player Steve Ott raced hydroplanes as a teenager.

Jay Fox

Jay Fox of Michigan was a champion junior racer before becoming a national and world champion tunnel boat racer. He has won at every level of competition he has raced. The boat he races today goes 100 mph faster than his junior class boat!

Valerie D'Agostino

Valerie D'Agostino of Maryland was inducted into the American Power Boat Association Hall of Champions as a junior class racer. Then she climbed the ranks of the adult classes. D'Agostino has already earned a national championship in adult hydroplane racing.

Valerie D'Agostino is the driver to beat in hydroplane racing.

The Youngest Champions

Garrett Armstrong of Wisconsin and Logan Sweeney of Ohio are the youngest boat racing national champions in history. They were both nine years old when they won their titles.

BUILDING AND CUSTOMIZING YOUR BOAT

You can learn a lot about racing boats by building one yourself. All you need is time, space in a garage or workshop, woodworking tools, and a good set of plans. Many race boat builders offer plans and kits for do-it-yourself boats. Some racers even go on to design their own boats.

Cool Paint Jobs

You can paint your boat however you want. Bright colors and graphics are popular. Pros

Joel Kiddy (222-F) and Becky Nichols, both of Florida, race creatively painted runabouts at the 2009 Southeast Divisionals in Jesup, Georgia. Kiddy won the title.

paint their sponsors' logos on their boats. Some drivers even paint their boats to look like powerful animals. A lot of kids pick out their own names, racing numbers, and colors. You can add decals to customize your boat even more.

If you do paint your boat, don't use too many coats of paint. The added weight can slow your boat down! Get an adult or an experienced boat racer to help you.

Colin Rucker shows off his runabout's paint job in Whitney Point, New York.

Safety Before Style

According to safety rules, you can paint the lower half of your helmet with your own design. The upper half of the helmet must be a bright orange or yellow color.

The Nydahls are a family of boat racers. Here (left to right) are Kurt, Pete, and Amy. Like his sister, Kurt entered the APBA Hall of Champions at the age of eleven.

FAMILY AND FRIENDS

There's a lot more to racing than just driving the boat. On a typical race weekend, drivers might spend only twenty minutes actually racing. Why go to that much trouble?

On Tour
Quality time with family and friends is an important part of boat racing. Kid racers get to

travel around the country with their families to race, to see sights, and to make new friends.

Go Team!

Family members work as teammates at the races. Parents might help their son launch his boat before a junior race. Later in the day, a daughter might fuel her dad's boat before an adult race. Racing teaches the whole family about teamwork, but spending time together is just as important.

Camping Out

Many boat-racing families camp out at the race site. They use their RVs to pull the boat trailer.

41

BOATBUILDING SCHOOL

A few years ago, the Hydroplane and Raceboat Museum in Kent, Washington, started a special boatbuilding project. The museum's members are usually busy restoring classic race boats. Instead, the museum teamed up with a local racing club to build junior class boats. They called it the J Project.

Before the decks can go on the boat, this builder must scrape off small bits of dried glue to give the boat a nice finish.

When all the woodwork is done, the boat is sealed with epoxy resin to protect the wood from the water. This is a job that the whole family can do together.

Spreading Success

First-time racers and their parents built their own boats with the help of museum staff and racing club members. The project was a great success. Similar programs have spread to the East Coast and Canada. A recent project in Maryland and Virginia produced eight junior race boats. That's enough new boats to run a whole race!

Helping Hands

Members of the Seattle Outboard Association helped out with the Hydroplane and Raceboat Museum's J Project. The Seattle Outboard Association is an example of a local racing club.

LEARN THE FLAGS

 **Green**—Flies three minutes before the start of the race; also means a race is under way

 **Blue and white**—Problems on the race course; continue with caution

 **Red**—Stop racing; be alert and watch for other signals

 **White**—Flies one minute before the start of the race; also flies when drivers reach their last lap

 Black—Return to pits (areas where racing teams work on their boats); the course is closed

 **Black and white checkered**—Finish!

GLOSSARY

amateurs—Beginners.

bow—The front end of a boat.

buoy—A brightly colored floating marker that shows turns on a racecourse.

classes—Groups of race boats based on engine size, boat type, and the driver's age.

cockpit—The part of a boat, car, or plane where the pilot and copilot sit.

currents—Movements of water in a certain direction.

deck—The top side of a boat, where people stand or sit.

drag—A force that slows something down in water or air.

hull—The bottom side of a boat.

inboard motor—An engine located inside the hull of a boat.

internal combustion engine—An engine that gets its power from burning fuel.

laps—Completed journeys around a track or course.

outboard motor—A detachable engine that clamps onto the back of a boat.

powerboat—A boat powered by an engine instead of sails or oars; also called a speedboat or motorboat.

propeller—A rotating device with blades that move a boat through the water. Also known as a prop.

restoring—Fixing something old to make it look new again.

rookie—A first-year boat racer.

sponsons—The two floats at the front end of a hydroplane that help keep the boat off the water.

straightaway—A long, straight part of a racecourse.

throttle—A hand lever that controls a boat's engine.

tides—Regular movements of water toward shore and away from shore.

transom—The back of a boat, where an outboard engine is mounted.

white water—Water with white-tipped waves.

FURTHER READING

Books

Dubowski, Mark. *Superfast Boats.* New York: Bearport Publishing, 2005.

Von Finn, Denny. *Hydroplanes.* Danbury, Conn.: Children's Press, 2008.

Web Sites

American Power Boat Association—*The official Web site of the APBA includes contact information for local racing clubs.* **<www.apba-racing.com>**

Hydroplane and Raceboat Museum—*Learn about the history of boat racing and the museum's many boatbuilding projects.* **<www.thunderboats.org>**

Hydroracer.net—*Check out discussion forums and news for boat racers.* **<www.hydroracer.net>**

INDEX